BASEBA...

GW00871582

If you have seen baseball games in the local park or on the television, and would like to know the basics of the sport, then this is the book for you. It takes you through the origins of the game, the skills involved, the equipment used and the organisation of baseball at a professional level in the USA.

Eddie Hufford is the Director of Physical Education at the American School in London.

BASEBALL

Eddie Hufford
Illustrations by Bob Harvey

CORONET BOOKS
Hodder and Stoughton

Dedicated to Helen LaFern, as promised
Copyright © 1987 by Victorama Ltd
Illustrations copyright © 1987
First published in Great Britain in 1987 by Coronet Books

British Library C.I.P.

Hufford, Eddie
  Baseball.
  1. Baseball – United States – History
  I. Title
  796.357'0973   GV863.A1

  ISBN 0-340-41893-1

Printed and bound in Great Britain for Hodder and
Stoughton Paperbacks, a division of Hodder and
Stoughton Ltd., Mill Road, Dunton Green, Sevenoaks,
Kent TN13 2YA. (Editorial Office: 47 Bedford Square,
London WC1B 3DP) by Cox & Wyman Ltd., Reading.
Photoset by Rowland Phototypesetting Ltd.,
Bury St Edmunds, Suffolk.

CONTENTS

INTRODUCTION

Baseball is a game traditionally played in the spring and summer in the USA, where it is considered to be the country's most popular game both from a player's and a spectator's point of view. But it is also played in at least 88 other countries around the world. Professional teams exist in Central and South America, Japan and Mexico, and the amateur game is played at various levels in all the countries considered to be baseball-playing nations. Although not included as an official sport in the Olympic Games, exhibition games were played in Los Angeles in 1984, with further ones being organised for Seoul, South Korea, in 1988.

The game is a team game with pre-planned strategies, which are constantly updated as the game progresses, depending on the relative state of the two teams involved. New strategies are given to the members of each team by a series of signals from the coach or other players.

Baseball is the only major game in the world in which a player is expected to hit a ball thrown towards him at 100 mph (160 km/h) with a rounded bat in a direction expected by the batter. Basically it is a game of throwing, catching, running, sliding and hitting. All these skills are refined to the highest level in the professional game; however, the simplicity of the basic game puts it within reach of everyone who enjoys a game with a ball and a stick-shaped bat.

ORIGINS AND HISTORY

The actual origins of baseball are not really known, but certainly games of stoolball, rounders and cricket have played their part in its make-up.

In America in 1839 a soldier called Abner Doubleday showed his friends how to play a game with a ball, bat and bases. Similar types of games had been played in the USA for several decades prior to this time under names such as Roundball, Sting Ball, Soak Ball, Burn Ball, Catapult Ball and One-hole Cat.

Then in 1846, at Hoboken, New York, Alexander Cartwright laid out and played the New York or Knickerbocker Game, which is the real basis of modern baseball.

In 1868 a cricket professional called Harry Wright came to Cincinnati, Ohio. He rapidly took to the game of baseball and organised the first openly-professional baseball club, the Cincinnati Red Stockings, which became nationally famous. When Harry Wright later moved to Boston, Massachusetts, he took the Red Stockings with him and used them to form another club which he called the Boston Red Stockings. Other cities' clubs imitated the way Wright's team dressed and named themselves after the colour of their stockings.

In 1876 Al Spalding and William Hulbert founded the National League of Professional Baseball Clubs, and over the next twenty-five years various teams joined it – and left it.

Various other rival leagues were subsequently formed. In 1882 the American Association came into being. Its clubs played their games on Sundays and charged spectators only half the National League entry fee. Then the Union Association in 1884, the Players' Association in 1891 and the American League in 1901 all came to challenge the National League as the organiser of baseball in the USA. In 1903, after failing to combine the National League and the American League into one organisation, the two league champions met in the first World Series. Other leagues were attempted, including the Federal League in 1914 and the Continental League in 1959, but both were doomed to failure by being outmanoeuvred by the National League and the American League.

In 1919 there was a scandal when eight Chicago White Sox players were bribed by gamblers to lose the World Series to the Cincinnati Reds. This resulted in the hiring of a Baseball Commissioner who from that time on became the supremo of the professional game in the USA. 1933 saw the first all-star game; 1935 the first floodlit night game; and in 1947 the first black major league player, Jackie Robinson, was allowed to play. Prior to this the Negro National League and the Negro Eastern League, formed in the early 1920s, had been the only places for black players to compete.

In the 1950s and 60s major league baseball expanded, and new teams were admitted to both the National and the American League. By 1969, with the advent of cheap, quick air travel, it was decided to divide each of the major leagues into two divisions.

The rules of the game have not changed drastically since the mid-1880s. The changes that have evolved have come about as a result of an attempt to make the game more exciting to player and spectator alike. In 1876 the following rules were in operation:

All pitching was to be underhand from a distance of 45 feet (13.7 metres).

The batter could ask for the type of pitch he wanted, i.e. high or low.

Nine balls were needed for a walk.

The batter was allowed two chances at the third strike.

The home team chose whether to bat first or second.

There were no bases, just stakes banged into the ground.

The major rule changes since then are shown below:

1877   The stakes were replaced with 15-inch (28-cm) square canvas bases all of which were in fair territory.

1880   Eight balls were needed for a walk.

1881   Fifty-feet (15-metres) pitching distance was introduced.

1882   Seven balls were needed for a walk.

1883   Any foul ball had to be caught on the fly to get the batter out.

1884   Introduction of overhand pitching. Six balls needed for a walk.

1886	Seven balls needed for a walk.
	New balls were to be available at any time from the umpire, not just at the end of the innings.
1887	The batter could no longer call for the type of pitch.
	Five balls needed for a walk.
	Four strikes needed for an out.
	The batter was entitled to walk to first base if hit by a pitched ball.
1888	Three strikes needed for an out.
1889	Four balls needed for a walk.
1891	Substitution allowed at any time.
1893	60 feet 6 inches (18.3 metres) pitching distance introduced.
	Pitcher's rear foot must be in contact with a plate measuring 12 inches (30 cm) by 4 inches (7.5 cm).
1894	Foul bunt is called a strike.
1895	Foul tip is called a strike.
	Infield fly rule introduced.
	Size of bat limited to 2¾ inches (70 mm) diameter.
	Pitcher's plate enlarged to 24 × 6 inches (60 × 15 cm).
1899	Balk introduced.
1900	Present home plate introduced.
1901	Two fouls count as strikes.
1904	The mound is limited to 15 inches (38 cm).
1910	Cork centred ball introduced.
1911	The wearing of white uniforms by the home team introduced.
1920	Spitball and other trick pitches outlawed.
	A faster and livelier ball was introduced. Because it was made from the same materials, this did not bring about a rule change. However, the new ball was more responsive and capable of being hit further, which attracted more spectators to the game.
1925	The home run distance set at a minimum of 250 feet (76 metres).
	The present soft cork centred ball introduced.
1934	Both major leagues use the same ball for the first time.
1973	Designated hitter introduced into the American League.

BASEBALL IN THE USA

Although baseball is played in at least 88 countries around the world, it is in the USA that the game has developed the most and the professional game is best established.

Throughout the USA, the game, at whatever level, is well organised. Neighbourhood teams are organised in Little Leagues which are closely controlled by the age of the players and the nature of the equipment used. T. Ball, for example, is a league in which the batter hits the ball from an adjustable rubber tee rather than trying to hit a moving pitched ball.

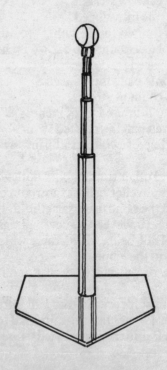

Fig. 1: *T. Ball Tree.*

Well over a million children play in Little Leagues every year until they reach the age of thirteen, when they can move into Pony League (PONY = Protect Our Nation's Youth) and Babe Ruth Leagues and finally the American Legion Leagues. All these organisations are for amateur players of the appropriate age level. Most high schools and colleges have their own teams, and it is from these sources that most of the professional players are drawn.

Since 1969 each of the major professional leagues has been divided into Eastern and Western divisions, each comprising a number of teams.

THE NATIONAL LEAGUE (FULL NAME THE NATIONAL LEAGUE OF PROFESSIONAL BASEBALL CLUBS)

Eastern Division	**Western Division**
Chicago Cubs	Atlanta Braves
Montreal Expos	Cincinnati Reds
New York Mets	Houston Astros
Philadelphia Phillies	Los Angeles Dodgers
Pittsburg Pirates	San Diego Padres
St Louis Cardinals	San Francisco Giants

THE AMERICAN LEAGUE

Eastern Division	**Western Division**
Baltimore Orioles	California Angels
Boston Red Sox	Chicago White Sox
Cleveland Indians	Kansas City Royals
Detroit Tigers	Minnesota Twins
Milwaukee Brewers	Oakland Athletes
New York Yankees	Seattle Mariners
Toronto Blue Jays	Texas Rangers

The minor leagues are also professional, and are affiliated to the major leagues but are self-governing. There are four categories of minor league associations.

Class AAA
Class AA
Class A
Rookie

All act as a 'farm' system for the major leagues.

In addition, there are summer leagues for college undergraduates organised and paid for by the professional clubs.

The baseball season starts with training in February and lasts eight months until mid-October. Spring training camps are held in Arizona and Florida and are used to get players fit and pick out possible new players. Each team plays a series of

1986 NATIONAL

	AT CHICAGO	AT MONTREAL	AT NEW YORK
CHICAGO		APRIL 15,17 AUG. 14*,15*,15*, 16*,17 SEPT. 15*,16*	JUNE 19*,20*,21,22 JULY 28*,29*,30* SEPT. 17*,18
MONTREAL	APRIL 24,25,26,27 JUNE 30 JULY 1,2 SEPT. 22,23		JUNE 23*,24*,25 AUG. 1*,2*,3 SEPT. 8*,9*,10*
NEW YORK	JUNE 27,28,29 AUG. 4,5,6,7 SEPT. 24,25	JUNE 16*,17*,18* AUG. 8*,9*,10 SEPT. 30* OCT. 1*,2*	
PHILADELPHIA	JUNE 16,17,18 AUG. 8,9,10 SEPT. 8,9,10	APRIL 22,23 JUNE 5*,6*,7*,8 SEPT. 26*,27*,28	APRIL 18*,19,20 JUNE 9*,10*,11* SEPT. 19*,20*,21
PITTSBURGH	APRIL 18,19,20 AUG. 11,12,13 SEPT. 19,20,21	JUNE 19*,20*,21*,22 JULY 28*,29*,30* SEPT. 17*,18	APRIL 21*,22* JUNE 13*,14,15,15 OCT. 3*,4,5
ST. LOUIS	APRIL 21,22,23 JUNE 13,14,15 OCT. 3,4,5	APRIL 18,19,20 AUG. 11*,12*,13* SEPT. 19*,20*,21	APRIL 14,16,17 AUG. 14*,15*,16,17 SEPT. 22*,23

exhibition games against teams from both leagues. These games do not count in league standings and are used to 'tune' the teams and get them game fit.

The playing season starts the first week of April and lasts until the first week of October. During that time each team will play about 160 games, half at home and half away.

Fig. 2: *Diagram of Schedules.*

AT PHILADELPHIA	AT PITTSBURGH	AT ST. LOUIS
JUNE 23*,24*,25* AUG. 1*,2,3 SEPT. 29*,30* OCT. 1* ·	APRIL 11*,12,13 JUNE 9*,10*,11* SEPT. 12*,13*,14	APRIL 8*,10 JUNE 5*,6*,7,8 SEPT. 26*,27,28
MAY 5*,6*,7* JUNE 13*,14*,15 OCT. 3*,4*,5	JUNE 27*,28*,29 AUG. 4*,5*,6*,7* SEPT. 24*,25*	APRIL 11*,12*,13 JUNE 9*,10*,11* SEPT. 12*,13*,14
APRIL 11*,12,13 AUG. 11*,12*,13* SEPT. 12*,13*,14	APRIL 8*,10* JUNE 5*,6*,7*,8 SEPT. 26*,27*,28	APRIL 24*,25*,26,27 JUNE 30* JULY 1*,2* SEPT. 15*,16*
	APRIL 24*,25*,26,27 JUNE 30* JULY 1*,2 SEPT. 22*,23*	JUNE 27*,28*,29 AUG. 4*,5*,6*,7 SEPT. 24*,25*
APRIL 14*,15*,16* AUG. 14,15*,16*,17 SEPT. 15*,16*		JUNE 23*,24*,25* AUG.8*,9*,10 SEPT. 30* OCT. 1*,2*
JUNE 19*,20*,21*,22 JULY 28*,29*,30* SEPT. 17*,18*	JUNE 16*,17*,18* AUG. 1*,2*,3 SEPT. 8*,9*,10*	

continued overleaf

13

	AT CHICAGO	AT MONTREAL	AT NEW YORK
ATLANTA	MAY 30,31 JUNE 1 AUG. 19,20,21	MAY 14*,15 JULY 17*,18*,19*,20	MAY 12*,13* JULY 10*,11*,12,13
CINCINNATI	MAY 26,27,28 AUG. 22,23,24	MAY 12*,13 JULY 10*,11*,12*,13	MAY 9*,10,11 JULY 7*,8*,9
HOUSTON	MAY 23,24,25 SEPT. 1,2,3	MAY 2,3,4 JULY 7*, 8*,9*	MAY 6*,7* JULY 3*,4,5*,6
LOS ANGELES	MAY 6,7,8 JULY 25,26,27	MAY 9,10,11 SEPT. 1*,2*,3*	MAY 27*,28*,29* AUG. 29*,30,31
SAN DIEGO	MAY 9,10,11 JULY 21,22,23	MAY 26*,27*,28* AUG. 29*,30*,31	JUNE 2*,3*,4* SEPT. 5*6,7
SAN FRANCISCO	MAY 13,14 JULY 17,18,19,20	JUNE 3*,4* SEPT.4*,5*,6*,7	MAY 30*,31* JUNE1 SEPT. 1,2*,3*
	13 SUNDAYS 0 NIGHT GAMES 2 HOLIDAYS (Memorial Day, Labor Day)	13 SUNDAYS 55 NIGHT GAMES 1 HOLIDAY (Labor Day)	13 SUNDAYS 49 NIGHT GAMES 2 HOLIDAYS (July 4, Labor Day)

In late July the pattern is interrupted for the all-star game, in which the best players from one league play the best players from the other. The profits from this game are donated to the Players' Pension Fund.

At the end of each season the teams that win each major

AT PHILADELPHIA	AT PITTSBURGH	AT ST. LOUIS
MAY 2*,3,4 JULY 7*,8*,9	MAY 26,27*,28* AUG. 22*,23*,24	MAY 23*,24*,25 AUG. 25*,26*,27*
MAY 14*,15* JULY 3*,4*,5*,6	MAY 23*,24*,25 AUG. 25*,26*,27*	MAY, 20*,21*,22 AUG. 29*,30*,31
APRIL 29*,30* JULY 24*,25*,26*,27	MAY 9*,10*,11 AUG. 18*,19*,20*	MAY 26*,27*,28 AUG. 22*,23*,24
JUNE 2*,3*,4* SEPT. 5*,6*,7	MAY 30*,31* JUNE 1 JULY 22*,23*,24*	MAY 13*,14 JULY 17*,18*,19,20
MAY 30*,31 JUNE 1 SEPT. 1*,2*,3*	MAY 13*,14* JULY 17*,18*,19,20	MAY 6*,7*,8 JULY 25*,26,27
MAY 27*,28*,29* AUG. 29*,30*,31	MAY 6*,7*,8* JULY 25*,26*,27	MAY 9*,10*,11 JULY 21*,22*,23*
13 SUNDAYS 62 NIGHT GAMES 2 HOLIDAYS (July 4, Labor Day)	13 SUNDAYS 63 NIGHT GAMES 1 HOLIDAY (Memorial Day)	13 SUNDAYS 57 NIGHT GAMES 1 HOLIDAY (Memorial Day)

league 'pennant' (the equivalent of the League Championship in British soccer) meet in the World Series to decide the World Championships. Until 1969 the team which won the greatest number of games in a season was declared the pennant winner, but since each league was divided into an Eastern and Western division, the pennant is decided by a play-off, the first to win three out of five games, between the two division winners in each league.

The World Series was first suggested by Barney Dreyfuss in August 1903. His idea was accepted by the President of the three-year-old American League and the World Series was born. Prior to this, the Temple Cup, started in 1894, was played for between the winner and runner-up of the National League.

The World Series is now played over seven games with the first to win four games being declared the winner. The teams move every two games to the opponent's stadium so that a fair share of home field advantage is possible.

WORLD SERIES WINNERS/LOSERS

1903 Boston	AL	5	Pittsburgh	NL	3
1904 No games					
1905 New York	NL	4	Philadelphia	AL	1
1906 Chicago	AL	4	Chicago	NL	2
1907 Chicago	NL	4	Detroit	AL	0
1908 Chicago	NL	4	Detroit	AL	1
1909 Pittsburgh	NL	4	Detroit	AL	3
1910 Philadelphia	AL	4	Chicago	NL	1
1911 Philadelphia	AL	4	New York	NL	2
1912 Boston	AL	4	New York	NL	3
1913 Philadelphia	AL	4	New York	NL	1
1914 Boston	NL	4	Philadelphia	AL	0
1915 Boston	AL	4	Philadelphia	NL	1
1916 Boston	AL	4	Brooklyn	NL	1
1917 Chicago	AL	4	New York	NL	2
1918 Boston	AL	4	Chicago	NL	2
1919 Cincinnati	NL	5	Chicago	AL	3
1920 Cleveland	AL	5	Brooklyn	NL	2
1921 New York	NL	5	New York	AL	3
1922 New York	NL	4	New York	AL	0
1923 New York	AL	4	New York	NL	2
1924 Washington	AL	4	New York	NL	3
1925 Pittsburgh	NL	4	Washington	AL	3
1926 St Louis	NL	4	New York	AL	3
1927 New York	AL	4	Pittsburgh	NL	0

1928 New York	AL	4	St Louis	NL	0
1929 Philadelphia	AL	4	Chicago	NL	1
1930 Philadelphia	AL	4	St Louis	NL	2
1931 St Louis	NL	4	Philadelphia	AL	3
1932 New York	AL	4	Chicago	NL	0
1933 New York	NL	4	Washington	AL	1
1934 St Louis	NL	4	Detroit	AL	3
1935 Detroit	AL	4	Chicago	NL	2
1936 New York	AL	4	New York	NL	2
1937 New York	AL	4	New York	NL	1
1938 New York	AL	4	Chicago	NL	0
1939 New York	AL	4	Cincinnati	NL	0
1940 Cincinnati	NL	4	Detroit	AL	3
1941 New York	AL	4	Brooklyn	NL	1
1942 St Louis	NL	1	New York	AL	1
1943 New York	AL	4	St Louis	NL	1
1944 St Louis	NL	4	St Louis	AL	2
1945 Detroit	AL	4	Chicago	NL	3
1946 St Louis	NL	4	Boston	AL	3
1947 New York	AL	4	Brooklyn	NL	3
1948 Cleveland	AL	4	Boston	NL	2
1949 New York	AL	4	Brooklyn	NL	1
1950 New York	AL	4	Philadelphia	NL	0
1951 New York	AL	4	New York	NL	2
1952 New York	AL	4	Brooklyn	NL	3
1953 New York	AL	4	Brooklyn	NL	2
1954 New York	NL	4	Cleveland	AL	0
1955 Brooklyn	NL	4	New York	AL	3
1956 New York	AL	4	Brooklyn	NL	3
1957 Milwaukee	NL	4	New York	AL	3
1958 New York	AL	4	Milwaukee	NL	3
1959 Los Angeles	NL	4	Chicago	AL	2
1960 Pittsburgh	NL	4	New York	AL	3
1961 New York	AL	4	Cincinnati	NL	1
1962 New York	AL	4	San Francisco	NL	3
1963 Los Angeles	NL	4	New York	AL	0
1964 St Louis	NL	4	New York	AL	3
1965 Los Angeles	NL	4	Minnesota	AL	3
1966 Baltimore	AL	4	Los Angeles	NL	0
1967 St Louis	NL	4	Boston	AL	3
1968 Detroit	AL	4	St Louis	NL	3

1969 New York	NL	4	Baltimore	AL	1
1970 Baltimore	AL	4	Cincinnati	NL	1
1971 Pittsburgh	NL	4	Baltimore	AL	3
1972 Oakland	AL	4	Cincinnati	NL	3
1973 Oakland	AL	4	New York	NL	3
1974 Oakland	AL	4	Los Angeles	NL	1
1975 Cincinnati	NL	4	Boston	AL	3
1976 Cincinnati	NL	4	New York	AL	0
1977 New York	AL	4	Los Angeles	NL	2
1978 New York	AL	4	Los Angeles	NL	2
1979 Baltimore	AL	4	Pittsburgh	NL	3
1980 Kansas City	AL	4	Philadelphia	NL	2
1981 New York	AL	4	Los Angeles	NL	2
1982 Milwaukee	AL	4	St Louis	NL	3
1983 Baltimore	AL	4	Philadelphia	NL	1
1984 Detroit	AL	4	San Diego	NL	1
1985 Kansas City	AL	4	St Louis	NL	3
1986 New York	NL	4	Boston	AL	3

PROFESSIONAL BASEBALL CLUB ORGANISATION

Many major league clubs are owned by individuals; others are owned by syndicates, but in both cases they are run as profit-making businesses, with each team worth tens of millions of dollars.

Each team has a general manager who is basically an executive vice-president. Other executives are responsible for personnel, public relations and promotions as well as the actual details of moving the team and its equipment from city to city for a whole season. This includes making all the travel and hotel arrangements.

An important part of the team's work involves scouting for prospective players. Twenty or thirty scouts are employed by each team to locate, check out and consider up-and-coming players from the minor leagues, colleges and high schools. The art of selecting the best prospects and actually signing them up for the team is very time consuming – but it can mean the team's future success or failure.

The squad of players is run by a manager, who is called the

head coach in other sports and who normally oversees the whole game operation as well as attending to details of the complete season, from training camp all the way to the World Series. The manager is assisted by four or five coaches who each have specific responsibilities for the actual game preparation and execution. One coach will be responsible for pitching, another for batting, another two for first and third bases and another for the warm up of relief pitchers in the 'Bull Pen'. This is an area at the back of the ball park where the pitchers warm up by practising their throwing.

Professional baseball players in the USA earn many tens of thousands of dollars. In addition to their salaries, most players get extra money for advertising and promoting products on TV and in newspapers. They have to work hard, for the season is very stressful with very few days off, and a lot of time being spent travelling between games in the different cities on the schedule. Depending on their abilities, particular roles in the team and their performance, players can continue to play well into their forties.

BASEBALL PERSONALITIES

With so many players and coaches being involved in the game over the last 100 or so years, choosing the most outstanding personalities is a difficult task. Nowadays the televising of games has brought the players right into people's homes, but long before television was available the greatest players and coaches were household names. Here are some of the all-time greats.

William Henry (Harry) Wright was the father of professional baseball. He was an Englishman who organised the first openly professional baseball club, the Cincinnati Red Stockings, in 1868.

Albert Goodwill (A.G.) Spalding was the father of the National League in 1876. He also is famous as the supplier of baseballs and baseball equipment, and the tradename of Spalding is still in use today.

Michael J. (King) Kelly in the 1880s was known as the 'King of the Diamond'. He played for Chicago as infielder, outfielder, pitcher, batter, base runner and slider. He was very flamboyant and a great favourite of the fans.

Charles Comiskey was the father of the American League. He played as a first baseman with the St Louis Browns and later founded the American League with Ban Johnson. He later went on to own the Chicago White Sox until he died in 1931.

Lewis Pages (Peter) Browning was the original Louisville Slugger. He did not actually invent the famous wooden bat of that name but had the first one made for him by John Hillerich of Louisville.

Cornelius McGillicuddy (Connie Mack) was a famous manager with the Philadelphia A's working right up to his retirement in 1950 at the age of eighty-eight. In his long career he won nine American League pennants and five World Series.

Joe Williams (the Texas Cyclone) was a famous black pitcher – probably one of the best ever. He was never allowed to play in the major leagues because of his colour.

Jay Hanna (Dizzy) Dean was one of the best-ever pitchers in the 1930s and '40s.

George Herman (Babe) Ruth was known as the 'one and only'. In the 1920s and '30s he was the greatest home run hitter who ever played in the major leagues.

Larry (Satchel) Paige was known as the **'Old Mose'**. He was a black player who only played in the major leagues when allowed to at the end of his career. In his fifties he played for the Cleveland Indians as a pitcher and was outstanding. He was probably at his peak the fastest pitcher ever.

Jack Roosevelt (Jackie) Robinson was in 1948 the first black player to be allowed to play in the major leagues.

Theodore Samuels (Ted) Williams is recognised as the real expert on the art of hitting. His baseball career spanned 21 years from 1939 to 1960.

Adrian Constantine (Cap) Anson was considered the best first baseman ever in the 1870s, '80s and '90s.

Roberto Walker Clemente was a Puerto Rican batter who was killed in an air crash whilst delivering relief aid to Nicaraguan earthquake victims in 1972. Clemente was also an excellent fielder, and was known to be one of the hardest throwers ever of a fielded ball.

Edward Trowbridge (Eddie) Collins who played between 1900 and 1932, was rated as the best second baseman ever. Although he threw a ball with his right hand he batted with his left.

Joseph Paul (Joe) DiMaggio played between 1936 and 1951. He was one of the best all round players ever. He holds the record 56-game hitting streak.

Ty Cobb in the 1880s was one of the game's greatest ever hitters.

Pete Rose (Charlie Hustle), has been playing since 1963. As player-manager with the Cincinnati Reds, established the all-time hitting record when he hit his 4,912th strike.

Willie Howard Mays Jr. was a spectacular fielder and batter in the 1950s, '60s and early '70s.

Mickey Charles Mantle was a specialist centre fielder in the 1950s and '60s who was also a powerful home run hitter and fast base runner.

Reginald Martinez (Reggie) Jackson was an exceptional home run hitter in the 1970s.

Undoubtedly other players will emerge as personalities both on and off the field. Those who are considered outstanding are elected to the National Baseball Hall of Fame, which, together with the National Baseball Museum, is situated in Cooperstown, New York. It was opened in 1939 and dedicated to the pioneers and great players of the game. Election of players and managers to the Hall of Fame is achieved in one of two ways. Some are chosen by a group of journalists from the Baseball Writers' Association of America; others are elected by a committee of veteran baseball players, each of whom has been out of the game for at least twenty years. Those elected have to have been involved with the game in the major leagues for at least ten years, and have to have been retired for five years or more before being considered.

STADIUMS

The stadiums used by the major league teams have changed in the last two decades. The geographic distribution of major league teams was unchanged between 1903 and 1952, but in the 1950s teams started to change franchises and both leagues expanded from eight to twelve teams. In 1977 the American League comprised fourteen teams.

All this was made possible by the greater use of long distance air travel, and by the desire of owners to make a profit. The televising of games, giving excellent coverage of all aspects of the sport, has made baseball the number one spectator sport in the USA.

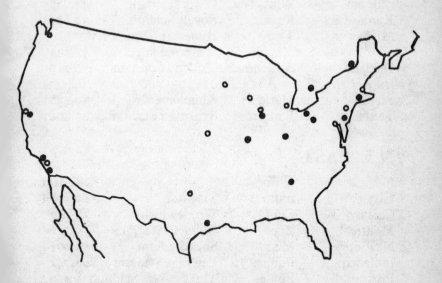

Fig. 3: *Map of USA showing Major League cities.*

A.L. EAST

City	Club name	Stadium	Stadium capacity
Baltimore	Orioles	Memorial Stadium	53,196
Boston	Red Sox	Fenway Park	33,583
Cleveland	Indians	Cleveland Stadium	74,208
Detroit	Tigers	Tiger Stadium	52,806
Milwaukee	Brewers	County Stadium	53,192
New York	Yankees	Yankee Stadium	57,545
Toronto	Blue Jays	Exhibition Stadium	43,737

A.L. WEST

City	Club name	Stadium	Stadium capacity
California	Angels	Anaheim Stadium	65,158
Chicago	White Sox	Comiskey Park	44,087
Kansas City	Royals	Royals Stadium	40,635
Minnesota	Twins	Hubert H. Humphrey Metrodome	57,545
Oakland	Athletics (A's)	Oakland Coliseum	50,219
Seattle	Mariners	Kingdome	59,438
Texas	Rangers	Arlington Stadium	43,508

N.L. EAST

City	Club name	Stadium	Stadium capacity
Chicago	Cubs	Wrigley Field	37,242
Montreal	Expos	Olympic Stadium	59,149
New York	Mets	Shea Stadium	55,601
Philadelphia	Phillies	Veterans Stadium	66,744
Pittsburgh	Pirates	Three Rivers Stadium	58,429
St Louis	Cardinals	Busch Stadium	50,222

N.L. WEST

City	Club name	Stadium	Stadium capacity
Atlanta	Braves	Atlanta – Fulton County Stadium	53,046
Cincinnati	Reds	Riverfront Stadium	52,392
Houston	Astros	Astrodome	45,000
Los Angeles	Dodgers	Dodger Stadium	56,000
San Diego	Padres	Jack Murphy Stadium	58,396
San Francisco	Giants	Candlestick Park	58,000

OFFICIALS

The umpire is the sole decider of the meaning and action of the rules of the game. Players and coaches are not allowed to argue about the judgement calls of the umpire, though they are allowed to question whether or not a particular rule has been applied. In major league and other important games a team of four officials covers the complete field. One is placed behind home plate, and one at each of the other three bases, and they communicate by means of a series of signals. Surprisingly, there are no universally accepted signals. Those shown opposite are those used at High School level.

The home plate umpire is the one who calls the balls and strikes after the ball has been pitched over the plate. He has a counter to keep an easy check on the count. In American League the umpire stands behind the catcher's head, whereas in the National League he looks at the plate from behind the catcher but by looking between the catcher and the batter. The home plate umpire wears protective gear very similar to that of the catcher. Umpires are traditionally dressed in dark blue, grey and black uniforms and are very unobtrusive when working.

Officials have to interpret the vast number of rules in the rule book and have a knowledge of case studies in which certain decisions were investigated before a consistent judgement was arrived at.

Several rules are not quite what they appear to be.

The Infield Fly rule states that if the ball is hit into the air in the infield and therefore can be easily caught, the batter is out even if the ball is not caught, when there are fewer than two outs and runners on first, second and possibly on third bases. The umpire will call out, 'Infield Fly, batter out if safe'. Runners are allowed to go to the next base at their own risk.

Fielders are not allowed to use a cap, glove or clothing not in contact with themselves to help field a ball.

If there is a tie in the runner getting to a base at the same time as the baseman receives the fielded ball whilst touching the base, providing the runner is forced to run, then the decision is given in favour of the runner. If the runner is not forced to run then the baseman cannot get the runner out by tagging the base but by tagging the runner before he reaches the base.

Fig. 4: *Umpire signals.*

1. Do not pitch
2. Play ball
3. Strike
4. Player is out
5. Fair ball
6. Delayed dead ball as for catcher obstruction
7. Foul ball
8. Runner is safe
9. Foul Tip
10. Infield Fly.
11. Time-out at ball dead immediately as for batter being hit by pitch or batted ball touched by spectator.

RECORDS AND STATISTICS

Anyone who can read can get a good idea of how any particular baseball game was played from the statistics which are kept and published as detailed reports in newspapers, magazines and books. The major league scores and statistics are published in national and international newspapers. In the UK *The Times* and the *Daily Telegraph* give a limited coverage of the final scores. The *International Herald Tribune* and *USA Today* (both available in the UK) give a wider coverage and use a box score system for reporting the game. This system was invented by H. Chadwick in the USA in the mid-nineteenth century and has been used ever since with only minor changes.

A typical box score looks like this.

Team A (A)	ab	r	h	bi	Team B (N)	ab	r	h	bi
Bergstrom ss	5	0	0	0	Marlow 2b	4	0	2	1
Rudolph cf	6	1	4	0	Wilson lf	4	0	0	0
Baldock 3b	6	1	2	3	Iacuessa 1b	4	0	0	0
O'Leary 1b	3	2	2	1	Carter cf	4	0	2	0
Lockwood rf	4	3	4	1	Ogle ss	4	0	1	0
Noble 2b	5	1	2	0	Adams 3b	3	0	2	0
Giardini lf	5	0	3	3	Balas rf	4	0	1	0
Fecher c	5	1	1	0	Watson c	4	1	3	1
Smith p	4	0	0	0	Dodson p	1	0	0	0
					Dorrian ph	1	0	1	0
Totals	43	9	17	8	Walker ph	1	0	0	0
					Harris ph	1	1	1	0
					Totals	35	2	13	2

Score at the end of each innings

Innings	1	2	3	4	5	6	7	8	9	Tot
Team A	0	1	1	0	2	1	0	2	2	– 9
Team B	0	0	0	0	1	0	0	1	0	– 2

E – Marlow. DP – Team A. LOB – Team A. 11. Team B. 8. 2B – Noble, Giardini, Balas, Carter. 3B – Rudolph, Lockwood, Harris. HR – Lockwood (7), Baldock (5) Watson (5). SB –

Rudolph 3, Fecher. S – Smith. SF – O'Leary.

	IP	H	R	ER	BB	SO
Smith (W, 5–4)	9	10	1	1	1	5
*Dodson (L, 6–4)	4	10	4	4	1	2
Woodford	1	1	1	0	0	0
Minter	2	2	1	1	1	2
Sinfield	1	2	2	2	0	1
Jimenez	1	3	2	2	1	3

*Faced 4 men in 5th

WP – Jimenez T – 2–14 A – 47, 354

To explain the system above you need to refer to the following key.

(A) = American League (N) = National League

Offensive record
ab = times at bat   r = runs scored   h = hits
bi = runs batted in

Fielding positions
cf = centre field   ss = short stop
rf = right field   1b = first base   3b = third base
lf = left field   2b = second base   c = catcher
p = pitcher   ph = pinch hitter

Defensive record
E = errors   DP = double play   HR = home runs
LOB = men left on   2B = two base hits   3B = 3 base hits
  base   S = sacrifices   TP = triple play
SB = stolen bases
SF = sacrifice flies
With HR is the season's total in brackets.

Pitcher's record
IP = innings   H = hits allowed   R = runs allowed
  pitched   SO = strike outs   BB = base on
ER = earned runs   L = losing pitcher   balls
  allowed
W = winning
  pitcher
In brackets are the pitcher's season win/loss record.
WP = wild pitch   T = length of game   A = attendance

Two not included in the example are HBP = hit by pitcher, pr = pinch runner.

The box score system looks complicated at first sight but it is really very simple.

Other statistics that are commonly in use are:

Batting average. This is where the ab (at bats) are divided into h (hits) to three decimal places.

Won–lost percentage. This is calculated by dividing the total number of games (wins plus losses, ignoring draws) into the number of wins.

Earned run average is calculated by dividing the number of innings pitched into the number of earned runs allowed and then multiplying the total by nine.

BASIC RULES AND PLAY

The rules of baseball are contained in a booklet of about 100 pages. The rules vary somewhat with the organisation involved, but the basic rules are common to all levels.

Baseball is played by two teams of nine players with a long, stick-like bat and a hard ball on a field. In one corner of the field there is a square marked on the ground, each corner of which is marked with a base fixed to the ground.

The members of each team take it in turns to attempt to hit the ball with the bat when the ball is thrown towards them by a member of the opposing team. If the ball is hit successfully in a certain direction then the batter attempts to run from base to base in an anti-clockwise direction.

The opposing team tries to stop the batting team from either hitting the ball or running around the bases in various ways:

■ Pitching the ball to the batter so deceptively that he cannot hit it.

Once the ball has been hit:

■ Catching it in the air.

■ Touching the runner with the ball while the runner is not actually touching a base. The ball is not allowed to be thrown at the runner in an attempt to accomplish this.

■ Getting the ball to a base before the runner gets to it. The runner has to be forced to run in order for this to apply.

THE FIELD

The playing field is a level piece of land about two acres (0.8 hectares) in area. In one corner of this field a square with sides 90 feet (27.4 metres) long and known as a diamond, is marked out.

A base is fixed to the ground at each corner of the diamond, that in the corner of the field being called the home plate, where the batter stands to hit the ball. In the centre of the diamond is the mound, from which the pitcher throws the ball. Once the ball has been hit into fair territory (the part of the field between lines drawn from home plate through the first and third bases), the batter runs in an anti-clockwise direction to first base, second base, third base and finally back to home plate.

The two teams take it in turn to bat and to field, the home team always fielding first. A team keeps batting until three players are out. Each team is allowed nine innings (unless fewer are agreed). If a game results in a tie at the end of nine innings, extra innings for each team are played until the tie is broken.

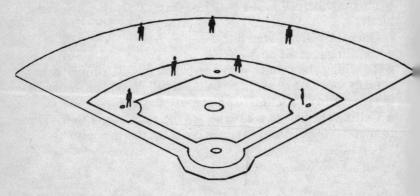

Fig. 5: *A baseball field, with players in usual positions. The three fielders at the top are the outfielders; the next four are the infielders.*

The fielding team is said to be the defensive team. Players in the defensive team except the 'battery' (the catcher and pitcher) are allowed to take up fielding positions anywhere in fair territory. The normal fielding positions are:

First base man
Second base man
Third base man
Short stop
Left field
Centre field
Right field

The battery (pitcher and catcher) have to be in their respective areas.

Once the fielding team is in position the umpire orders the first batter to get into the batter's box and the game to begin. The pitcher throws the ball towards home plate from the mound. If the batter thinks he can hit the ball, he swings the bat at it. If the ball is hit and goes into fair territory, the batter has to drop the bat and run to first base. If the ball is caught by a fielder before it hits the ground, the batter is out. Assuming this doesn't happen, the batter can continue to run from first to second to third base and then finally to the home plate only if he thinks he can get to the next base without being tagged with the ball. If the batter decides it is too risky to run to the next base he can stop at any base and is safe as long as he is actually touching the base. Every time a runner successfully goes around all four bases a run is awarded.

The batter has to judge if the ball pitched towards him is going to be a strike or a ball. A strike is a pitch over home plate that is between the batter's knees and armpits in height.

Fig. 6: *Strike zone*.

Whether the batter actually swings the bat at a strike or not it is still counted as a strike if declared so by the umpire. A batter is allowed three strikes in which to hit the ball. If he fails to do this, he is struck out.

If a ball is pitched outside the strike zone it is declared a ball. If a batter swings the bat at a ball pitched outside the strike zone it becomes a strike even if he fails to hit it. The umpire calls out the number of balls and strikes so that the count is known. If a batter is pitched four balls he is allowed to walk to first base without being liable to being tagged out. If a pitched ball is hit into foul territory (the part of the field outside the first and third baselines) it is still declared a strike but the batter cannot run. If a strike into foul territory is caught on the fly (in the air) a batter is out. If a strike into foul territory is the third strike for a batter, providing it is not caught, the batter is not out and is allowed any number of foul strikes as third strikes.

The pitcher obviously tries to pitch the ball to the batter in such a way that it is declared a strike without the batter hitting it. Alternatively he may pitch it in such a way as to make the batter hit it for a catch or to a specific part of the field.

A batter who hits the ball anywhere inside fair territory is allowed to run to as many bases as he wishes. If he hits the ball over the boundary within fair territory it is declared a home run and he is allowed to touch all four bases and score one run without the risk of being put out. If a ball bounces in fair territory and then becomes unplayable because it is in the spectators' area, the batter is allowed to move two bases. A runner on base is allowed to advance to the next base on his own initiative. If he can do this without being tagged he is said to have 'stolen' a base.

The four basic ways in which an offensive player can be put out are:

■ Failing to hit three strikes.

■ Hitting a pitched ball which is caught in either fair or foul territory without it touching the ground.

■ Being tagged by a fielder holding the fielded ball whilst not on a base.

■ Being forced to run to a base and having a fielded ball reach the base first.

Every time a runner reaches home plate having touched first, second and third bases, a run is scored. It does not matter if a runner has stopped at any of the bases on the way round.

Once three players are out of a team the innings is ended. The fielding team then becomes the batting team and the batting team becomes the fielding team. The batting order of the nine players is declared at the start of the game and this must be followed throughout the entire game. If, at the end of an innings, batter no. 6 is the last to bat, at the start of the next innings batter no. 7 will be first to bat. If a batter is out the first time during an innings, providing the innings is long enough for his turn to come again, then he must bat.

Substitutions are allowed at any time, but the player coming into the game must bat at the same number as the player he is replacing. The player going out of the game is not allowed to re-enter. In American League a designated hitter is allowed to substitute for the pitcher without the pitcher being barred from the fielding side of the games, but designated hitters are not allowed in the National League.

EQUIPMENT

DIAMOND

The diamond's sides are 90 feet (27.4 metres) long. The base lines are constructed from cinders, as frequently is the whole of the infield. The outfield is generally grass or Astroturf. All lines are painted on to the surface.

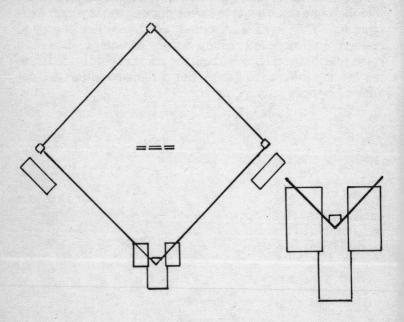

Fig. 7: *Official measurements for the diamond are shown (left) and home plate area is shown in detail (right).*

HOME PLATE

The home plate is a five-sided solid white rubber plate which has removable spikes to fix it to the ground. The edges of the plate are tapered to avoid injury to a sliding runner. The whole of the plate is in fair territory.

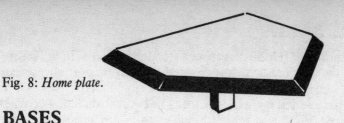
Fig. 8: *Home plate.*

BASES

First, second and third bases are made of white canvas and stuffed with a soft material. They are anchored to the ground and are in fair territory. Recent developments have brought forward a new sort of base which is tapered like the home plate but made of a pre-formed durable synthetic material.

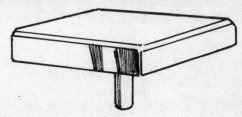
Fig. 9: *Base.*

THE PITCHER'S MOUND

The pitcher's mound is 9 feet (2.7 metres) in radius and 10 inches (27 cm) above the rest of the field. It has a flat top containing the pitcher's plate, which is a piece of rubber fixed to the ground. In major leagues this plate is square and in other leagues it is rectangular.

Fig. 10: *The pitcher's mound.*

THE BALL

All hard balls (baseballs) are of a standard pattern. In the centre is a soft cork ball which is covered with layers of rubber, wool yarn and cotton yarn before finally being covered with white cow hide which is glued in place. The cover is also stitched with 108 red double stitches. Smaller balls are used for Little League, and for some practice and beginners' games a rubber baseball (more durable, less hard) is produced. Up until 1920 the baseball was less lively than it is now, which meant it was harder to hit long distances. In 1920 the owners of the major league clubs introduced the new, livelier ball in an attempt to attract more spectacular play. This did not mean a change in the rules, rather a change in the method of playing.

Fig. 11: *The ball.*

THE BAT

Bats vary in length between 2 ft 6 in and 3 ft (76 cm and 91 cm) and weigh between 2 lb and 2½ lb (0.90 kg and 1.13 kg). Special small bats are made for Little League players.

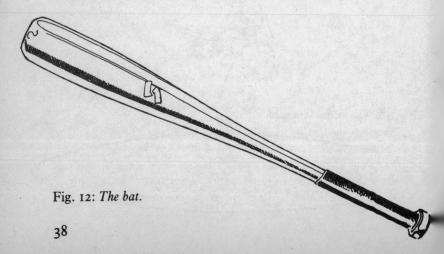

Fig. 12: *The bat.*

Bats are either made of wood – either hickory or white ash – or aluminium. Wooden bats tend to crack or break, so major league players (who are only allowed to use wooden bats) can get through up to 100 bats in a season. Their bats are individually made. Most bats for other leagues are made of aluminium which last much longer than wood but initially they are much more expensive than a wooden bat.

UNIFORMS

Baseball uniforms have not changed a great deal since the game began, but they are now made from stretch polyester or acrylic fibres and are generally more snug fitting than their predecessors. The uniform consists of a cap, a short-sleeved top, a pair of knickerbocker-style knee-length trousers, stirrup socks, special shoes and an athletic supporter (jockstrap).

THE CAP

The peaked baseball cap is a very widely used design and is fully adjustable. Few players ever play without a cap for the peak protects their eyes from the sun's glare. Many players also wear flip-up sun glasses when fielding to guard against glare.

Fig. 13: *Cap.*

THE SHIRT/TROUSER UNIFORM

Depending on the location of a game, the time of year, the time of the game and the personal preferences of the players, other clothing (T shirt/sweatshirt/undervest) will be worn in addition to the actual uniform. Home team uniforms are always white whilst away uniforms are either grey or coloured. Major league teams display their nicknames on their home outfits, and each player has his number and surname on the back of his shirt. When playing away the name of the team's home city is always on the front of the shirt.

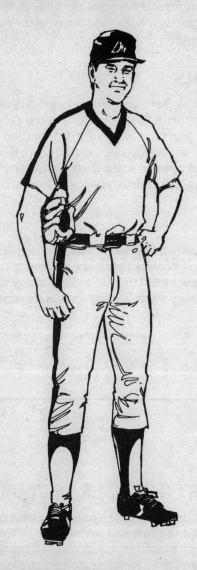

Fig. 14: *Shirt/Trousers.*

SOCKS

Baseball socks are socks without feet. They are like a pair of stirrups which go under the instep of the foot. Usually players wear a pair of sports socks under the stirrup socks for comfort.

Fig. 15: *Socks.*

WARM-UP JACKETS

All players have a warm-up jacket to wear whilst warming up and while sitting on the bench in the 'dug-out'. The jacket normally has the name of the team on it as well as the player's name and number.

Fig. 16: *Jacket.*

SHOES

Traditional shoes for baseball are made of black leather. (Good quality ones from kangaroo leather.) Modern shoes resemble trainers. On the soles of the shoes are blunt, flat steel cleats (spikes) for use on grass and cinder fields, or a special moulded sole pattern for use on Astroturf and cinder fields.

Fig. 17: *Shoes.*

GLOVES

Modern gloves bear very little resemblance to those used before the Second World War. Modern fielding gloves are now bigger and more flexible, with the catching being done away from the padded palm of the hand, in the pocket at the top of the glove.

The three basic fielders' gloves are for the first baseman, pitcher and outfielder. Each type of glove has its speciality features designed to assist the fielder in his particular part of the game. The glove is worn on the hand that is not used for throwing, i.e. a right-handed thrower wears the glove on, and therefore catches with, his left hand. Gloves are made of leather or vinyl and need to be broken in before being used. Every player has his own method of doing this and players are normally quite possessive about their glove.

The rules do not insist that players wear a glove, though at the speed at which baseballs are thrown or hit it is most strongly advisable to do so. In practice very few players ever play without a glove.

The catcher's glove is different to the other fielders' gloves.

It is much more padded and rounded and is designed to take the sting out of the pitched throws.

Batters wear a glove similar to a golfing glove on one or both hands to help with the grip. Originally players rubbed a pine tar rag on the handle of the bat to improve the grip.

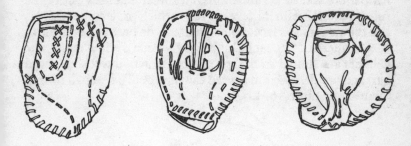

Fig. 18: *Gloves.*

CATCHER'S PROTECTIVE EQUIPMENT

The catcher is the only player allowed to wear pads, which are designed to cover the exposed parts of the body when in a normal crouched receiving position. They are light-weight and flexible to allow the great mobility and speed required by the catcher as well as letting him throw effectively. His head is protected by a helmet (worn back to front) and a padded wire face mask.

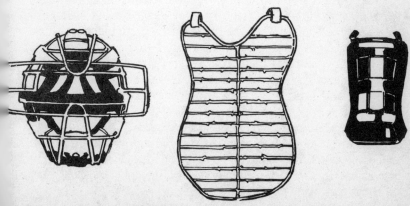

Fig. 19: *Catcher's equipment.*

Most players also wear a protective cup which fits inside the jock strap.

HELMETS

All batters and base runners have to wear a helmet under the rules. Batters' helmets have ear flaps which protect the temples and the sides of the face. Once a batter is on base and becomes a base runner he can change his helmet for one without flaps. The helmets are similar in design to a construction worker's 'hard hat' and are designed to spread the impact of a baseball hitting them at 100 mph (160 km/h).

Fig. 20: *Helmet*.

SKILLS

As stated in the introduction the game of baseball is one of throwing, catching, hitting, running and sliding. Each skill has had many books written about it, but the basics are outlined below.

HITTING/BATTING

Hitting a baseball with the bat is probably the most difficult skill of the entire game. It is an individual skill and the techniques used vary with every player.

Fig. 21: *Batting.*

When a ball is pitched from 60 feet (18 metres) away at 100 mph (160 km/h) it takes less than half a second to travel that distance. The batter only has a quarter of a second in which to sum up the type of delivery, decide what he is going to do and then swing if he decides he can hit it. A lot of hitting technique requires determination, concentration and confidence.

A batter's job is to hit the ball safely. By standing in a comfortable stance and watching the ball all the time it is possible to watch it, a batter can learn to swing only at pitches that are strikes. The batter stands sideways on to the pitcher, with the weight on his rear foot. The ball should be hit in front of the plate not over it. As the bat is swung towards the ball the batter's weight is shifted onto the front foot by taking a small step to meet the ball. The object is to hit the ball squarely so the swing should be level with the elbows which should be kept away from the body.

Fig. 22: *Batting sequence*.

Even the best batters only hit the ball 40 per cent of the time. Since the batter's main job is to avoid striking out and to advance runners around the bases it is essential that batters only attempt what they are capable of or follow the instruction of the coach.

Seventy-five per cent of all batters are right-handed, and right-handed batters fare better against left-handed pitchers. Similarly, left-handed batters do best against right-handed pitchers. Some batters, like Mickey Mantle, are 'switch hitters' which means they can bat equally well with either hand and can change according to the pitcher on the mound.

46

Fig. 23: *Batting grips.*

BUNTING

Bunting is a form of batting which is performed in a very limited and controlled way. It is a calculated move to out-manoeuvre the fielding team in order to advance runners and/or score a run.

Fig. 24: *Bunting.*

Basically once the ball has been pitched the batter squares up to the delivery by turning his feet and body through 90 degrees. He holds the bat in front of him with a shoulder width grip and lets the ball hit the bat and deflect in the direction he wants. This is normally away from any fielder or the base to which he is hoping to advance a runner.

BASE RUNNING

The world record for running the 360 feet (109.6 metres) around the bases is 13.3 seconds. This means that the type of running required is an explosive sprinter's action. It is very rare for a runner to score a home run by running the bases non-stop. Most home runs are scored by hitting the ball out of the ball park over the boundary fence or after a good hit and a fielding error. The sprint action is, however, the action needed to run successfully between the bases.

Once the weight is on the front foot in the batting action and the ball has been hit into fair territory, the batter's job is to get to first base. The forward motion has been started by the transfer of body weight in the batting action so the next step is the start of the sprint action which includes the discarding of the bat.

The use of the arms in sprinting is paramount. The legs will only move as fast as the arms are being moved in a balanced sprint action.

Whilst running towards first base the runner has to be aware of the first base coach, who will be signalling what to do. The options will be as follows:

■ Run straight to the base, touching it with a foot on the way and continuing down the first base line. A runner does not have to stop at first base providing he does not try to miss it out by turning straight towards second base.
■ Slide in to first base to try to avoid a tag from the first base man.
■ Swerve out to run through first base on the way to second base.

Once a runner is on a base, he looks for signals from the coaches as to how to proceed. He looks for these signals while safely touching the base. Once the pitcher has the ball the runner should lead off but only go as far as he can safely get back from if the pitcher decides to try a pick off attempt.

A runner waiting on second base should try to read the signals between the pitcher and the catcher and relay them to the man coming up to bat. The runner approaching second base has to make his own decisions on how to proceed. The runner coming into third base looks for similar signals as the runner coming into first base, but the signals will come from the third base coach. The runner coming into home looks at the on-deck batter for a signal as to whether to slide or not.

SLIDING

The basic skill is a bent leg slide, which begins about 10 feet (3 metres) from the base. The runner takes off on the most comfortable leg which becomes the bent leg and he slides on the outside of the bent leg foot and his lower back. The top leg is straight about 6 inches (15 cm) above the ground.

Fig. 25: *Sliding*.

The bent leg slide can be used to stop overrunning a base by using the top leg as a brake at the last moment, which results in the runner returning to a standing position in contact with the base.

Other slides are:
■ Take off slide, which is aimed at the baseman rather than at the base.
■ The hook slide, which is used to evade attack.
■ The head first slide which is the best one for covering the last few feet in the least possible time.

PITCHING

Pitching is the most important element in the game. Mathematically the odds in a game of baseball are very much in favour of the batter. During the course of a nine innings game, the pitcher has to get twenty-seven players out, whereas a game can be won with just one run.

The overarm throwing action is an unnatural action. Not all pitchers use overarm, some use three-quarter or side-arm actions. Pitchers develop a repertoire of deliveries so that the strain of throwing is not always on the same part of the arm and body. By varying the deliveries the pitcher also tries to outwit the batter so that he does not actually hit any ball pitched towards him.

The pitcher has a lot to think about when he is ready to deliver. He has to look for signals from the catcher and decide upon the type of delivery depending on the batter's weaknesses and strengths, as well as the catcher's signals. He has to look for base runners trying to steal a base and he has to be aware of the count (number of strikes and balls pitched).

Fig. 26: *Pitching sequence.*

The pitcher can vary:
- The speed of the ball.
- The placing of the ball within the strike zone i.e. high or low, inside or outside.
- The trajectory of the ball by curving the delivery or making it change direction. He tries to disguise his intentions but at all times tries to limit the batter's options.

The three main pitches are:
- A fast ball, which is easily thrown to a particular spot. It has to be fast to be useful.
- A curve ball, which is a ball spun by the pitcher which breaks down and away from the batter as it approaches the plate.
- A change-of-pace ball, which is delivered the same as a fast or a curve ball, but is slower than the fast ball and not recognised as easily as a curve ball.

Other pitches used are:
- The slider, which is a cross between the fast and the curve ball. It curves away from a straight delivery but does not drop like a curve ball.
- A screw ball, which is a reverse curve ball and is often thrown by a left-handed pitcher to a right-handed batter.
- A knuckle ball, which is thrown with the knuckles or finger-tips gripping the ball. It is unpredictable and can be a problem for the catcher.
- A sinker, a type of fast ball or slider with little horizontal break but a definite downward movement.

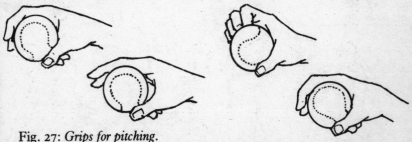

Fig. 27: *Grips for pitching.*

Any trick delivery such as a 'spit ball' is not allowed. Some pitchers still try to cut, rough up or dampen the surface of the ball in order to gain an advantage. If they are caught attempting this, they are thrown out of the game.

Once the pitcher has taken his stance on the mound prior to

pitching he must place one foot (the right foot for· a right-handed pitcher) actually on the pitcher's plate or rubber. If there are no runners on base he uses the full wind-up – i.e., the stretching of his body and arms to get him in the best position to throw the ball at its hardest. If runners are on first or second bases or both, the pitcher, in order to prevent a steal (the term applied when the base runner 'leads off' prior to the pitch of the ball and succeeds in getting to the next base without being tagged), restricts the wind-up. If he stretches he must return to a normal pitching position and pause, with the ball at chest level, before pitching. A balk is called if he fails to do this, which results in all runners advancing one base. When a runner is leading off a base in order to steal, the pitcher will throw to the base in an attempt to tag the runner out. He must take a deliberate step in the direction of the base when attempting this or a balk is called.

Sometimes a pitcher will deliberately 'walk' a batter by intentionally pitching four balls outside the strike zone. This will be done to prevent an in-form batter from actually hitting and therefore possibly scoring. By deliberately walking the batter, the best the man can do is get to first base.

Pitchers also have to field balls to the infield, pick up bunts, back up plays at third base and home and sometimes make the play (become the base man) at first or home.

Fig. 28: *Pitcher becoming first baseman.*

CATCHING

The catcher is the fielder who is behind the home plate. He is the player who signals the strategies to the fielding team, having decided upon the abilities of the batter and the positions of the runners.

Fig. 29: *Catcher's signals.*

The catcher's glove is used as a target for the pitcher to aim at.

Fig. 30: *Catcher's stance.*

The catcher must be able to catch all types of balls whether pitched or fielded. He must also be able to throw well to prevent stolen bases and he must also be able to field bunts and slow hit balls and get the ball to a base ahead of the runner. If a batter hits the ball high into the air near the batter's box, whether into foul or fair territory, the batter will be out if the ball is caught. Usually this is done by the catcher having discarded his mask and sometimes his helmet in order to see the ball in the air. The catcher is also the baseman for the home plate and he must be able to receive fielded balls and either tag the base or tag the runner. This can be a very rough position since with the runner intent on scoring he will frequently slide in such a way as to get the catcher off balance and therefore make him unable to tag him.

INFIELDERS

Infield players are the first base, second base, third base and short stop.

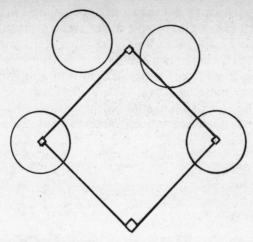

Fig. 31: *Infield responsibilities*.

The baseman does not field touching the plate but needs to be within reach of it either to beat the runner to it, having fielded the ball, or to beat the runner to it and receive a fielded ball from elsewhere. When merely tagging the base, the baseman usually stands inside the plate so that a runner sliding in does not collide fully with him. When tagging a runner it is necessary for the baseman to be in a position to touch the runner prior to the runner touching the base.

Fig. 32: *Baseman*.

The first baseman is allowed to wear a bigger glove than the other fielders. He should be able to get his foot on and off the base as quickly as possible, and be capable of catching some extremely hard hit or thrown balls.

Second baseman needs a strong throwing arm, whilst the third baseman must be brave, agile and remain calm under pressure. The short stop should be the best all-rounder. He needs to be fast, consistent and able to read the situation quickly.

Fig. 33: *Batter/runner being out by the base being tagged.*

OUTFIELDERS

Left field, centre field and right field are the outfielder positions.

Fig. 34: *Outfielder.*

Outfielders should be able to throw a long way with accuracy. If a player is not strong then an infielder not involved in the play can be used to relay the ball from the outfielder to the baseman.

The outfield usually shifts as a unit depending on the batter. They should be able to field both ground balls and fly balls and throw them to the baseman as speedily as possible. Usually the ball is thrown to the base ahead of the runner.

STRATEGIES

In the professional game in the USA teams are only allowed a playing squad of twenty-five players in the dug-out. Usually this is made up as follows:
ten pitchers
six or seven infielders
five or six outfielders
three catchers

The coach sets up the batting order according to the relative strengths of his team.

The lead-off batter is chosen for his ability to be fairly certain of getting to first base by either being 'walked' or by being able to hit away from the fielders.

The second batter should have the same skills but should be quicker between the bases and good at hitting to right field.

The third, fourth and fifth batters are the big hitters, with the fourth being the 'clean-up man' who can hit a home run or at least bring in one or all of the base runners.

The sixth batter needs to be reasonably strong; **the seventh, eighth and ninth** are the weakest, with **the pitcher** probably being ninth.
   Various strategies can be used both in offence and defence. Here are a few of those most widely used.

OFFENSIVE STRATEGIES

Hit and run
The batter should hit the ball on the ground irrespective of where it is pitched. It should be hit between the first and second basemen but behind the runner going from first to second base. The object of the play is to advance the runner an extra base and to protect him from the double play.

Run and hit
If the pitcher is behind on the count then the batter tries to hit the ball anywhere. The runner on base is signalled to be on the move and the batter hits the ball if it is in the strike zone.

Hitting the ball to the opposite field
This play needs a lot of bat control but it is effective in breaking up the double play.

Getting a run by sacrificing an out
The batter deliberately hits the ball to an infielder knowing that he is going to be out as a result but also knowing that the runner from third base will score a run.

Bunt and run
This play is normally tried with no outs and a fast runner on first base. It is used to advance the runner to third base. The ball is normally bunted down the third base line.

Squeeze play
This is an offensive situation favoured by the New England coach John Carr. The squeeze is normally attempted in a late innings with a runner on third base, one player out and the score being a tie or very close.

The idea is to allow the runner on third base to get home and therefore score. The batter bunts the ball (see below) in such a way that the runner can get home before the bunted ball is fielded and thrown to home plate. In a 'suicide squeeze' the third base runner starts from home plate as soon as the pitcher has committed himself to pitch and before the batter actually bunts the ball. If the bunt goes in the wrong direction the third base runner can very easily be out. In a 'safety bunt' the runner only sets off if the bunt has been put on the ground.

Bunting
This is a way of hitting the ball without taking a swing at it. This play is not normally used in the early innings of a game, though occasionally it is used as a surprise tactic. In order not to make the bunt too obvious a drag or push bunt is done, which can deceive the fielding team and allow the batter to get on base. With a 'drag' bunt the batter does not square up to the pitched

ball but makes as if to swing the bat (as in a well-hit strike) but instead hits the ball with the stationary bat shortly after the pitch has begun. With a 'push bunt' the batter performs a similar trick at the end of the swing, with the same motive and result. Sometimes a batter will assume the bunting position and then change his mind and swing at the ball.

Stealing

Stealing is explained on page 60. It allows a team to advance a base without a sacrifice and it keeps a pitcher on his toes. Single steals are normally only attempted when the team is ahead or the game is tied with the count being three balls and one strike or three balls and two strikes (full count).

A double steal occurs when two runners start at the same time from first and third bases hoping that the play to second base to get the runner from first base out will allow the runner from third base to score a run.

The secret of good baseball, both offence and defence, is for a team to have an effective system of signals between coaches and players. These signals should be simple so that every member of the squad can fully understand them. There are several methods of signalling:

Flash   a signal which is given very quickly.
Hold   this is held for several seconds.
Block   utilises different blocks of the body.
Combination needs more than one action to mean anything.
Rub off   cancels the previous signal.
Word   the coach actually speaks to the player.

Any signal system only works if the player looks for the signal at the right time and in the right place.

DEFENSIVE STRATEGIES

Good defence is a combination of good pitching and tight, sound fielding. The actual fielding positions vary with every batter, the score, the innings and the runners on base.

Various strategies are employed to achieve sound, tight fielding all of which depend on team work and an understanding of each player's responsibilities and capabilities.

Relays

When the ball is hit to the outfield either the short stop or second baseman will move out to receive the throw in from the outfielder and relay it to the correct position.

Cut-offs

This play is used to prevent a runner from taking an extra base if no play occurs at the home plate by diverting a fielded ball from one direction and getting it to a base to stop a runner advancing. The play is usually organised by the catcher. If a ball is batted to the outfield with a runner in a scoring position (i.e. on second base), then the baseman not involved in a possible play (first or third baseman) runs to a position in the infield, about 10 yards (9 metres) in front of the home plate, in line with the throw from the outfield. If the runner is going to score then the catcher tells this fielder to intercept the throw and get it to second base in order to cut off the runner going from first base to second base.

Run down play

This is used to tag a runner who is trapped between two bases. Normally, in this situation, the runner returns to the base he has left, so the fielder runs towards the retreating runner down the base line faking a throw hoping that the runner will change direction and run towards him. If the runner does not change direction the baseman should come out from the base to 'sandwich' the runner, receive the ball and tag the runner before he can get safely back on the base.

With runners on first and second bases the infield have to do some quick thinking and moving. Fielders must be prepared for the bunt whilst others should be prepared to cover the bases left unoccupied by the fielders of the bunt.

Double and triple plays

This is where by quick fielding and an agreed system of where the fielded ball is to be thrown, two, in the case of the double play, offensive players are put out. Normally in a double play a fielded ball will be passed to second base, which is tagged before the runner from first is safe and then the ball is passed by the second baseman to first base to get the batter/runner out before he has covered the 90 feet (27.4 metres) to the base.

Signalling

From the bench or the dug-out the coach (usually the head coach or manager) is able to see the fielding positions and patterns. He uses signals to move the fielding places according to the state of the game, (the score, the count) and the position and strengths of the batter and the runners on base.

Frequently the players will talk to each other as to who is actually going to catch or field the ball as well as where the ball should be thrown to. If a fly ball is hit between the infield and the outfield, generally the outfielder will catch it because he is able to keep his eye on the ball the whole way whilst running in a forward balanced position. The infielder should not try to interfere or attempt to catch the ball whilst retreating backwards.

The signals between the catcher and the pitcher are extremely important defensively. A typical system of signalling the type of pitch required is as follows:

Fast ball   one finger
Curve ball   two fingers
Change-up ball   three fingers
Any other pitch   four fingers

If a runner is on second base the catcher will try to conceal the signal so that the runner will not be able to relay the message back to the batter.

Fig. 35: *Scooping the ball on the move.*

The catcher will also signal where in the strike zone he wants the pitch in the following manner:

Low and outside   palm down/away from batter
Low and inside   palm down/towards batter
High and outside   palm up/away from batter
High and inside   palm up/towards batter

If the pitcher disagrees with the catcher's signal he gives a slight shake of the head. If they cannot agree they will confer together at the mound.

CATCHING AND THROWING

When fielding, every player on the defensive squad has to be able to catch and throw the ball whilst on the move.

Fig. 36: *Catching*.

The secret of successfully catching a ball as a fielder is to keep the eye on it all the time. The feet have to be moved to get the body into a balanced position, and once the ball is in the glove, the glove must be closed, even if it means using the other hand in order to do so and keep the ball in the glove.

Fig. 37: *Baseman avoiding a sliding runner.*

The hand without the glove is the throwing hand. The ball can be transferred from the gloved hand into the throwing hand in one swift movement. In order to throw most effectively the distance to be covered has to be considered. If the short stop only has to throw the ball 20 feet (6 metres) to the second baseman then a gentle underhand toss is sufficient. If the third baseman has to throw the ball to first base ahead of the runner, then an overhand power throw is called for. For any throwing action the opposite leg to the throwing arm should be forward and the legs, trunk, arms, wrist and fingers are used to propel the ball to its target.

INJURIES

In such a fast-moving game some injuries are inevitable, but many can be avoided by good conditioning, preparation and warm-up. Each team has a trainer who is responsible for treating injuries. In the major leagues, the players are such a valuable asset that a team doctor is available at all times.

Any injury, especially to a pitcher, can seriously affect a team's performance. Each training room contains whirlpool baths which are used to ease swellings caused by injury. Since pitchers always have rest days between games there is time for minor injuries to be treated.

Occasionally injuries to the hamstrings (the muscles at the back of the thigh which end in tendons behind the knees) and knees occur. Normally rest and ice applications help, and strapping of the affected area with tape can allow a player to perform despite a slight injury.

Most players suffer burns from sliding on the cinder area at the bases or when fielding on Astroturf. These are normally not serious, just uncomfortable. Basemen get injuries from being hit by runners' shoes, despite the fact that the cleats are not sharp or pointed, or by being in a collision with a runner when they are both trying to reach a base.

Injuries to fingers, even when wearing a glove, do occur and occasionally fingers are broken.

The use of batting helmets, catcher's mask and pads have reduced the number of serious accidents resulting from being hit with a ball either pitched or thrown from a fielder.

BASEBALL IN EUROPE AND THE UNITED KINGDOM

The game in Europe is an amateur one. The two main countries involved are the Netherlands and Italy, though the game is played in most other European countries by ex-patriot Americans as well as local nationals.

In the United Kingdom the game was at its zenith around the time of the Second World War. Now it is growing in popularity again, and is played in many parts of the country either at club level, school level or Little League level.

The game is controlled in the UK by the British Amateur Baseball and Softball Federation. Any local Sports Council office (telephone number will be in any local directory) will be able to give the name of either the nearest local club or the address of the current Secretary of the National Federation. Both these contacts will be able to give information about the game at local and national levels.

Adult leagues are organised and play in the summer (basically during the cricket season). Teams are very pleased to welcome spectators and often local newspapers advertise the time and place for the games.

Some schools have teams and the National Federation has a schools section. Again, the local Sports Council office will be able to provide information to those who are interested.

American communities in the United Kingdom organise Little League baseball and softball leagues for children from the age of eight to fifteen. Any interested spectators or players are normally welcomed.

The International Schools Sports Tournament organisation which arranges games and tournaments in many sports includes in its programme a baseball season between Easter and mid-

June. With five member schools in the United Kingdom as well as others all over Europe and the Middle East the standard of play is good for school level.

The professional game can be followed by tuning into AFN (American Forces Network) radio programmes during the regular baseball season. AFN is receivable on several wavelengths on the medium waveband. Live games are broadcast sometime between 6.00p.m. and 2.00a.m. British time depending on where in the USA the game is being held. Channel 4 television have started to bring highlights of the World Series to Britain and this is expected to continue in years to come.

Any keen fan can subscribe to *The Sporting News* which publishes a weekly newspaper covering all the major American sports in some depth. Since this has to be posted from the USA it usually arrives several weeks after the date of publication. It is a serious reference journal, and a useful supplement to the daily newspapers mentioned earlier in the book.

The Sporting News is obtainable from:
The Sporting News
100 Stadium Drive
Marion
Ohio 43305
USA

Other suppliers of serious baseball literature, statistics and up-to-date information are:

Baseball America
PO Box 2089
Durham
North Carolina 27702
USA

Preview Publishing
PO Box 19200
Seattle
Washington 98109
USA

Sportspages
Sports Bookshop
Shopping Centre
Cambridge Circus
Charing Cross Road
London WC2

SOFTBALL

The game of softball is virtually the same as baseball, except for the size of the ball. The softball is not soft but is of similar construction to a baseball, though 12 inches (30 cm) in circumference. Larger (16-inch/40-cm) balls are available but are harder to throw because of their greater size.

Softball is traditionally the game that girls and women play in the USA. Its skills and strategies are almost identical to baseball, with a few exceptions. The major difference lies in the pitching rules, and therefore skills. In softball all pitching has to be underhand, and it is governed by two rules. The slow pitch rule states that the pitched ball must have a noticeable arc on its trajectory of at least 3 feet (1 metre). This means that the ball is pitched fairly slowly which makes it generally easier to hit than a baseball. In fast pitch softball, the pitcher winds up by swinging the ball in a circular motion at the side of the body, but the ball has to be released in an underhand throw.

The size of the diamond is smaller than in baseball, the base-lines being 60 feet (18.3 metres) long, and the pitcher's plate being 46 feet (14 metres) from the home plate.

Many schools in the United Kingdom play a form of slow pitch softball in physical education classes, often using no fielding gloves, no catcher's equipment and no proper bases.

A few club teams exist in several parts of the country and information on them can be obtained from your local Sports Council office.

GLOSSARY

Appeal: a question by the defensive team about a rule violation, which is not made by the umpire.

Around the horn: when a fielded ball is thrown firstly to third base, then to second and finally to third base. During this process a double play is gained for the defensive team by the ball reaching the base (actually touching the base) ahead of the advancing runners at second and third bases.

Bag: the actual canvas base fixed to the ground at first, second and third bases.

Bail out: when the batter moves out of the way quickly to avoid being hit by a pitched ball.

Balk: a movement by the pitcher in the wrong direction, when a runner is on base. All runners and the batter can advance one base following a balk.

Battery: the catcher and the pitcher.

Bean ball: an illegal pitch aimed at the batter's head.

Blank: what a pitcher is said to do to a team when it fails to score.

Bleachers: the unshaded seats beyond the outfield which are the cheapest for spectators.

Bleeder: a lucky hit which eludes a fielder.

Blooper: a short fly ball that lands between the infield and the oufield.

Blow up: to suddenly lose control of one's skills.

Bobble: the fumbled fielding of a ball.

Bottom: the innings for the home team.

Bull pen: the area where relief pitchers warm up.

Bunt: a batted ball not swung at.

Bush league: a league far below the standard of the major league.

Cage: the backstop behind the catcher. It may be portable.

Called game: a game shortened by the umpire.

Choke up: to grip the bat above the end, which is the normal position.

Clean-up position: fourth to bat.

Clothes line drive: a hit which travels about 10 feet (3 metres) off the ground to the outfield.

Count: the number of balls and strikes pitched to a batter.

Crowding the plate: standing very close to home plate whilst batting.

Dead ball: a ball temporarily out of play because of the suspension of play by the umpire.

Designated hitter: in the American League, a player who hits for the pitcher but never fields.

Double: a two-base hit.

Double header: two consecutive games between the same two teams on the same day at the same ball park.

Double play: a play when two players are out.

Dug-out: a recessed covered area for each team on either side of the diamond.

Duster: a pitch thrown close to the batter's head.

Error: a fielding mistake.

Fair territory: the part of the field inside the first and third baselines.

Fat pitch: an easily hit ball.

Fly ball: a ball hit into the air.

Forced out: when a runner is out by the base being tagged because he has to advance.

Foul territory: the part of the field outside the first and third baselines.

Fungo: a hit ball in practice thrown into the air by the batter.

Gopher ball: a hit which is intended as a home run.

Grand slam: a home run with all the bases loaded.

Ground rule double: limits the runner to two bases because the ball has gone into the spectators' area.

Grounder: a hit which lands on the ground in the infield.

Hit the dirt: to slide into a base.

Homer: a home run.

Hot corner: third base.

Keystone: second base.

Knocked out of the box: to relieve a pitcher during an innings.

Lead off man: the first batter in the line up.

Line drive: a hard-hit, low ball.

Line up: the batting order of each team.

On deck: a circle near the batter's box for the next batter to wait in.

Passed ball: a pitched ball which eludes the catcher.

Perfect game: when a pitcher allows no runner to get to first base.

Pinch hitter: a batter who substitutes for the man due to bat.

Pinch runner: a substitute sent in to run for a runner already on base.

Pitchout: when the pitcher deliberately throws the ball outside the strike zone. This is done either to 'walk' a good batter or to allow the catcher to get the ball quickly and throw it to a base to get out a runner attempting to steal.

Pivot foot: the foot of the pitcher which is placed on the pitching plate and not allowed to move. It is the foot on the same side as the hand used for pitching.

Portsider: a left-handed pitcher.

Pull hitter: a batter who hits the ball to the side of the field away from the batting hand.

Rain check: a token given to spectators if a game is postponed due to rain which allows access to the ball park in the future free of any extra charge.

Rally: when a losing team suddenly begins to level the score towards the end of the game.

Rhubarb: an explosive argument involving several players.

Riding the bench: a player who is not in the regular line up.

Rookie: a first-year player.

Rosin bag: a bag kept on the mound containing rosin to improve the pitcher's grip.

Rubber arm: a term for a pitcher who has great stamina.

Seventh innings stretch: by standing at the start of the seventh innings to stretch tired limbs the fans are supposed to bring the team good luck.

Shake off: the slight shaking of the head by the pitcher if he disagrees with the catcher's signals.

Shutout: a game when one team fails to score.

Single: a one-base hit.

Slugger: a consistent long hitter.

Southpaw: a left-handed batter or thrower.

Sprayhitter: a batter who hits to all parts of the field.

Tag: when a fielder either touches a runner or a base whilst holding the ball.

Take a pitch: to allow a pitcher to throw a strike without trying to hit it.

Top: innings for an away team.

Triple: a three-base hit.

Triple play: the fielding of a ball which results in three offensive players being put out.

Walk: an unimpeded advancement of one base by all base runners, including the batter, after a set amount of balls not considered to be strikes.

Wild pitch: similar to a passed ball, but which is caused by the pitcher.

GENE KLEIN AND DAVID FISHER

FIRST DOWN AND A BILLION

"My two happiest days were the day I bought the San Diego Chargers and the day I sold the San Diego Chargers"

Gene Klein

In 1966, having made a fortune from nothing, Gene Klein bought the American Football team the San Diego Chargers.

FIRST DOWN AND A BILLION portrays two tumultuous decades in the National Football League and exposes the business battles between fellow owners, agents, players and the union. He hired and fired head coaches, drafted and traded players, survived the first major drug scandal in pro Sports, and helped negotiate the largest television contract in Sports history.

FIRST DOWN AND A BILLION is both an intriguing book for the businessman and a fascinating insight for the sportsman and will prove invaluable whether you're into fitness or finance.

A Royal Mail service in association with the Book Marketing Council & The Booksellers Association.
Post-A-Book is a Post Office trademark.

MIKE BREARLEY

THE ART OF CAPTAINCY

English cricket's most successful captain of recent years, Mike Brearley was also the most thoughtful and articulate of captains.

Now he has written:

'The most perceptive book ever likely to be written on cricket captaincy'

The Times

'A masterpiece of its kind'

The Sporting Life

'An indispensible book for cricket lovers'

Melody Maker

'Enjoyable and laudable ... the tactical wisdom comes spiced with so many amusing stories'

The Times Literary Supplement

'Fascinating'

Morning Star

'Brilliant'

Mail on Sunday

'It can be admired with almost no reservations. Its anecdotes are vividly indiscreet, its judgments frequent and fearless ... and yet the persuasive tone is genial and relaxed'

New Society

CORONET BOOKS

ALSO AVAILABLE FROM
HODDER AND STOUGHTON PAPERBACKS